Jackie's GIFT

by Sharon Robinson

illustrated by
E. B. Lewis

VIKING
An Imprint of Penguin Group (USA) Inc.

STEVE STARED UP at the tall evergreen. It was Christmas Eve day and he was helping his neighbors, Mr. and Mrs. Robinson, decorate their tree.

Mrs. Robinson hung gold, blue, green, and red ornaments, while little Jackie tossed tinsel on the lower branches.

"Pass me that string of lights, Steve," Mr. Robinson called from behind the tree that dwarfed his nearly six-foot frame.

Steve hastily gathered up the lights. "What a swell-looking tree!" he said.

"We had to have the biggest one in the lot," Mr. Robinson replied, smiling. "This is our first Christmas in Brooklyn, after all."

Steve couldn't believe his luck. He was standing here decorating a tree with his new neighbor, the Brooklyn Dodgers' famous second baseman, Jackie Robinson!

Steve Satlow lived for baseball. Nine months earlier, he had
been eagerly awaiting the start of the 1948 baseball season and
the Brooklyn Dodgers' return to Ebbets Field. But on Tilden
Avenue, where Steve lived, another bit of news had all the
neighbors abuzz: a black family was moving into the two-story
brick house two doors down from the Satlows.

Over dinner one night, Steve's dad told him that some of their neighbors had tried to stop the black family from moving in. A few families had sent around a petition, but they couldn't get enough signatures.

"We refused to sign, of course. I can't believe that any other Jews would sign that petition either," Mrs. Satlow said.

"Why?" asked Steve.

"Well," Mr. Satlow explained, "do you remember that your Bubbe and Zayde, my parents, left Russia for America when they were in their twenties?"

"Sure," said Steve. "They still talk with accents."

"They had to flee from people who were treating them badly just because they were Jewish. They'd heard that in America, people of different races and religions live together in peace—that's why they came here."

"If only America really were color-blind," added Mrs. Satlow.

"All I know is that Jackie Robinson is the best player the Dodgers have ever had, black or white," Steve said.

"It's funny you should mention Jackie Robinson," said Steve's dad.

"Why's that?"

Mr. Satlow smiled. "Because that's just who's going to be our new neighbor."

"You've got to be kidding!" Steve shouted. Never in his wildest dreams had he imagined living two doors down from Jackie Robinson!

For days, Steve couldn't stop peeking out the front
window, waiting for the Robinsons' moving van.

When the van finally arrived, he rode his bike up and down
the street, hoping to catch a glimpse of the baseball player.

He saw men carrying lots of boxes.

He saw a lady he figured must be Mrs. Robinson, holding a
little boy's hand.

But there was no sign of his hero.

The next morning, Steve and his mother picked cherries from the tree in their yard and brought them to the house at 123 Tilden. As his mother and Mrs. Robinson chatted about the neighborhood, Steve peered around the doorway into the house. But he still didn't see Mr. Robinson.

Steve perked up when Mrs. Robinson asked him, "Are you a Dodgers fan?"

"You bet. A Jackie Robinson fan, too!"

Mrs. Robinson laughed. "Good. You'll have to go to a game with Jackie Jr. and me soon."

Steve left the Robinsons' house beaming. He hoped Mrs. Robinson really meant what she said.

On a warm, sunny afternoon a few weeks later, Ebbets Field was packed. From their seats right behind home plate, Steve, Mrs. Robinson, and Jackie Jr. cheered loudly when number 42 came up to bat. Steve was sure Jackie could hear them.

The bases were loaded.

Dodgers fans were on their feet screaming, "Jackie! Jackie! Jackie!"

Jackie lifted his big bat high above his shoulder.

Steve held his breath as the ball sailed over the plate.

"Ball!" the umpire shouted.

Jackie relaxed his stance and took a few practice swings. He bent low, lifted his bat, and waited. The pitcher reared back, stepped forward, and unleashed a thundering fastball. Jackie swung hard.

The ball and bat exploded with a *CRACK!*

The ball *flew* over the center field wall.

Mrs. Robinson and the boys jumped almost as high!

Best of all, Steve got to walk home from the game with none other than Jackie Robinson himself. It was the most exciting day of Steve's life.

Now, months later, Mrs. Robinson switched on the Christmas tree lights. They sparkled red, yellow, and green.

"Wow!" Steve cried.

Jackie Jr. clapped and laughed as his father lifted the angel to the very top of the tree.

"Have you decorated your tree yet?" Jackie asked Steve as Mrs. Robinson handed them both mugs of hot chocolate.

"We don't have one," Steve said with a heavy sigh.

The Robinsons shared a puzzled look.

Mrs. Robinson cleared her throat. "Are you enjoying the school vacation, Steve?"

Steve grinned. "You bet!"

The subject of the Christmas tree seemed to be forgotten. Soon, Steve thanked the Robinsons and left to join his friends, who were sledding in the park.

Later that afternoon, Jackie Robinson knocked on the Satlows' door with a Christmas tree under his arm.

"My goodness, Jackie Robinson! What a surprise!" Mrs. Satlow cried as she opened the door. "It's so nice to finally meet you. Steve talks about you nonstop. Come in, please."

"Steve was at our house earlier," Jackie said as he stepped into the living room. The tree was still under his arm. "He was helping us decorate our tree and, well . . ." He hesitated. "He said that you didn't have one. So, I hope you don't mind—I bought him a tree."

Sarah covered her mouth with her hand, trying to hide her shock. "Oh, my," she whispered. "I don't know what to say. It's so kind of you to think of us."

After Jackie left, Steve's mother walked around the living room, not sure what to do.

"What's that tree doing here?" Steve's father asked when he came home.

"Jackie Robinson bought it for Steve," she said. "Can you believe it?"

"Didn't you tell him that we don't celebrate Christmas?" Mr. Satlow asked.

"I didn't know what to say. I know his wife, Rachel, but it was the first time I'd met Jack." Mrs. Satlow sank into the couch shaking her head. "Imagine what my mother will say!"

"I know what she'll say, Sarah.
She'll say, '*Oy vey!*'"

Steve ran in, breathless from sledding. His eyes widened when he spotted the tree.

"Did you tell Mr. Robinson that you wanted a Christmas tree?" his father asked sternly.

"No!" Steve exclaimed. "I just told him we didn't have one. Did Jackie bring that tree for me?"

"It's Mr. Robinson to you, Steve," his father corrected.

"Can we keep it, Dad? Please?"

"It was a mistake," explained Mr. Satlow. "Mr. Robinson didn't understand that we don't celebrate Christmas."

"But it's just a tree," Steve protested.

"It's more than a tree. It's a religious symbol, just like our menorah is for Hanukkah," Mr. Satlow told him.

"But, Dad," Steve said, "the tree is a gift. You always tell me to accept gifts in the spirit that they're given. Right?"

Before Mr. Satlow could reply, the doorbell rang. Steve's mother answered the door and greeted the Robinsons warmly. She waved them inside.

"Jack told me that he bought Steve a tree, so we brought over some extra lights and ornaments," Mrs. Robinson began, then stopped. "What's wrong?" she asked.

"Rachel, do you remember at Easter when you asked what church we belong to, and I told you that we're Jewish? That also means we don't celebrate Christmas. We celebrate Hanukkah," Steve's mother explained gently.

"Instead of having a tree, we light candles in a menorah," added Mr. Satlow.

"I grew up in an Orthodox Jewish home," Mrs. Satlow said. "My mother would be shocked to see a Christmas tree in our house!"

Mrs. Robinson looked at her husband in horror. The room was silent.

Steve tried not to laugh. All the adults looked so
serious. But when he caught his mother's eye, she started
to giggle and soon they all joined in.

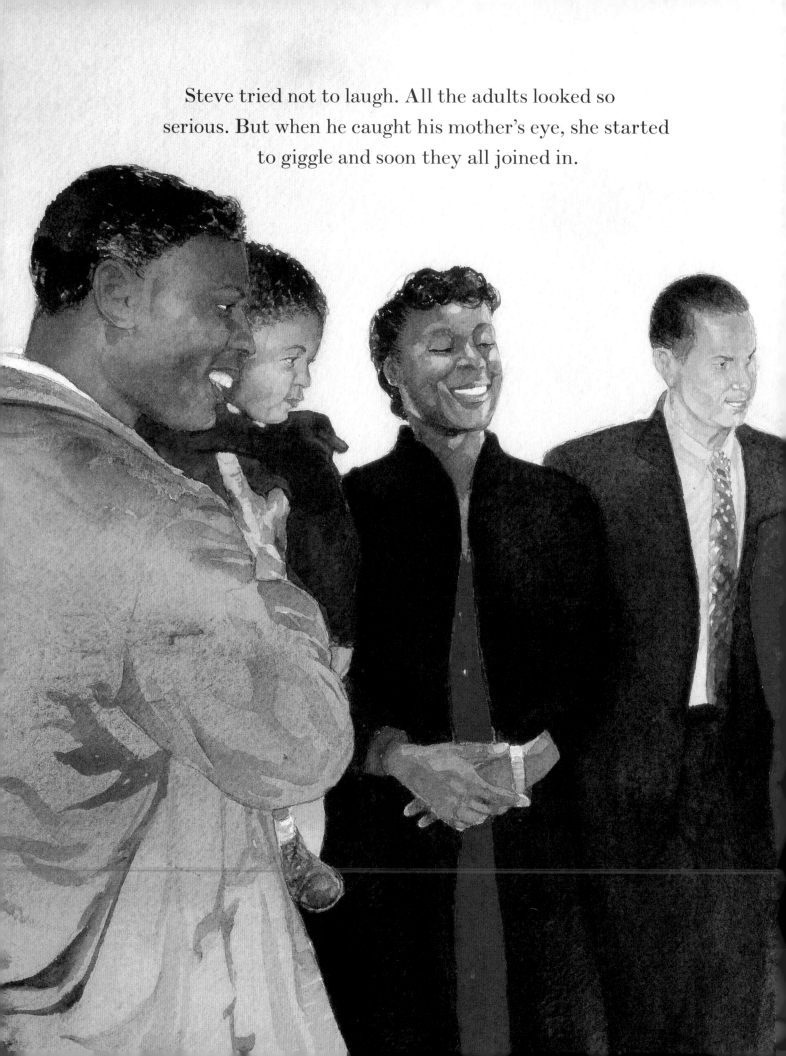

"What a mess I've made of things! Please forgive us," Jackie said, chuckling.

"We're so embarrassed," Mrs. Robinson added.

"Please don't be!" Mrs. Satlow said. "You were being generous to our son. There's no harm in that."

"So, Dad?" said Steve, looking to his father hopefully. "What do you think?"

Mr. Satlow smiled down at his son.

"Okay," he declared. "This Jewish family is going to have a Christmas tree *and* a menorah this year."

And they did.

Author's Note

Jackie's Gift is based on a true story. My parents, Jack and Rachel Robinson, moved to 123 Tilden Avenue in the Flatbush section of Brooklyn in 1948. After a very successful first season with the Brooklyn Dodgers, my father began his second season in a slump that lasted until mid-June when he hit a grand slam.

The Satlows lived just down the avenue from my parents. This was before my younger brother David and I were born, when my older brother, Jackie Jr., was just a toddler. In real life, Archie and Sarah Satlow had three children: Steve and his sisters, Sena and Paula. Our families formed a bond many years ago that has lasted a lifetime. In the years since then, Steve and I both lost our fathers, as well as Jackie Jr. and Paula.

The Christmas tree story was always a big hit in our family. A few years ago, I met one of my favorite illustrators, E. B. Lewis, at a children's book festival. E. B. asked me if the fabled Christmas tree story about my father was really true. I told him it was, and that evening, we agreed to work together to share it with children.

Steve delighted in helping me retell a cherished piece of his childhood as much as Sarah Satlow and my mother enjoyed sharing their memories with me. Now I hope our story will inspire families for generations to come to look beyond race and religion and into people's hearts.

To Rachel Robinson, my extraordinary mother and best friend,
and to her dearest friend, Sarah (Satlow) Cymrot.—S.R.

To the Haddonfield Friends School, with gratitude for all your help.—E.B.L.

VIKING
Published by Penguin Group
Penguin Young Readers Group, 345 Hudson Street, New York, New York 10014, U.S.A.
Penguin Group (Canada), 90 Eglinton Avenue East, Suite 700, Toronto, Ontario, Canada M4P 2Y3 (a division of Pearson Penguin Canada Inc.)
Penguin Books Ltd, 80 Strand, London WC2R 0RL, England
Penguin Ireland, 25 St Stephen's Green, Dublin 2, Ireland (a division of Penguin Books Ltd)
Penguin Group (Australia), 250 Camberwell Road, Camberwell, Victoria 3124, Australia (a division of Pearson Australia Group Pty Ltd)
Penguin Books India Pvt Ltd, 11 Community Centre, Panchsheel Park, New Delhi – 110 017, India
Penguin Group (NZ), 67 Apollo Drive, Rosedale, North Shore 0632, New Zealand (a division of Pearson New Zealand Ltd.)
Penguin Books (South Africa) (Pty) Ltd, 24 Sturdee Avenue, Rosebank, Johannesburg 2196, South Africa

Penguin Books Ltd, Registered Offices: 80 Strand, London WC2R 0RL, England

First published in 2010 by Viking, a division of Penguin Young Readers Group

1 3 5 7 9 10 8 6 4 2

Text copyright © Sharon Robinson, 2010
Illustrations copyright © E. B. Lewis, 2010
All rights reserved

LIBRARY OF CONGRESS CATALOGING-IN-PUBLICATION DATA
Robinson, Sharon, date–
Jackie's gift / by Sharon Robinson ; illustrated by E. B. Lewis.
p. cm.
Summary: When young Steve, who is Jewish, tells his new neighbor, Jackie Robinson, that his family does not have a Christmas tree,
Jackie brings one to his neighbors, not knowing that they celebrate Hanukkah instead of Christmas. Based on a true story.
ISBN 978-0-670-01162-9 (hardcover)
1. Robinson, Jackie, 1919–1972—Juvenile fiction. [1. Robinson, Jackie, 1919–1972—Fiction. 2. Christmas—Fiction. 3. Christmas trees—
Fiction. 4. African Americans—Fiction. 5. Hanukkah—Fiction. 6. Jews—United States—Fiction. 7. Race relations—Fiction.]
I. Lewis, Earl B., ill. II. Title.

PZ7.R567683Jac 2010   [E]—dc22   2009048435

Manufactured in China   Set in Scotch Roman   Book design by Nancy Brennan